J-ROCK PUBLISHING
BOOKS FOR YOUNG ADULTS

WWW.JROCKPUBLISHING.COM
JASENSOUSA.NET
MYSPACE.COM/JASENSOUSA

Selected Poems

of

Jasen Sousa

Age

17-24

Other books
by
Jasen Sousa

Life, Weather

A Thought and a Tear for Every Day of the Year

Close Your Eyes and Dream With Me

Almost Forever

A Mosaic of My Mind

....

Selected Poems
of
Jasen Sousa

Age

17-24

Photographs
By
Alex Foster, Auther Roberson, Alfred E. Soccorso,
Edmund Sousa, Jasen Sousa and Tom Westcott

Editing Team

Lisa Johnson, Rene F. LaMorticelli, Ann Mento, Debbie Senesi,
Rose Soccorso, Darlene Sousa, Jasen Sousa

Selected Poems
of
Jasen Sousa

Age
17-24

Edited by Rene F. LaMorticelli, Ann Mento, Debbie Senesi, Rose Soccorso, Darlene Sousa, Jasen Sousa

Book Design by Dime Designz and Lisa Johnson

Photographs by Alex Foster, Auther Roberson, Alfred E. Soccorso, Edmund Sousa, Jasen Sousa and Tom Westcott

J-Rock Publishing and Dime Designz
In affiliation with Eudimeonia Entertainment

J-Rock Publishing
45 Francesca Avenue
Somerville, MA 02144

Library of Congress
Cataloging in Publication Data
ISBN 978-0-9714926-5-3

Manufactured in The United States of America

Printed in Somerville, Massachusetts

For Chris Ormond

INTRODUCTION

I was asked by my friend Auther once, what my secret is that keeps me going? As far as I know, this is the only life I will get to experience. There is no guarantee of an afterlife, a Heaven, or a Hell. With this being my belief, I try to do everything I physically can before I am gone forever.

I have flirted with the idea of being crazy before, but I have come to find out I am not. I lived through many days with images of my own death bouncing around in my head. I believe that they are there for a reason. Without them I would have never been able to accomplish what I have.

When I became lazy and wanted to relax, I would remind myself there is no time for that. I'm 24-years-old and I have more passion and energy inside of my body today than I will at any other point in my life. Every day that passes I become weaker physically, so I cannot take days off.

Think for a moment, what is lost throughout the course of a day?
I can recall many poems I wrote that would have never taken form if I were to succumb and simply say, "I'll just do that tomorrow." For me, my tomorrow was always today. For that reason and that reason only, is why I have more accomplished today than the average person will have completed by tomorrow.

When you live by this philosophy each day, things tend to pile up. I can remember that warm August night when I was 17-years-old and wrote my first poem. Now it's 2008 and I have written over a thousand poems, compiled five books of poetry that have been published, and have many more in my secret vaults which are completed.

When you begin living and planning far into the future, that's where you end up. There are many projects I am working on that might not get to see the light of day until long after I am gone from this earth. I wish I could share my creations with the world while they are being born in my brain, but I realize that sometimes that cannot be. I relate this feeling to having great news, you want to call everyone and tell them, but no one answers. No one is around.

You have to wait for the right time when people are ready to listen, and right now my audience is not ready to listen. I am not going to say I am ahead of my time because of my thoughts and ideas, that's for my fans and the critics to determine, but I will say I am ahead of my time because I live in a different time period than those who walk beside me.

The year is 2008, I operate and live somewhere around 2015. So, what keeps me going? The answer is simple, I am already gone. I do not live in your world, I live in mine and I wait here patiently and alone until someone finds my coordinates and decides to pay me a visit. My question to you is, what are you waiting for?

SOMERVILLE - LINE
DO NOT
ENTER
SOMERVILLE

CONTENTS

I

II

III

IV

V

Selected Poems

of

Jasen Sousa

Age

17-24

I

The underground sound.
Crowds stand up to hear him play,
the train kills his voice.

A STREET IN SOMERVILLE

My street
is located near a high land,
on opposite sides
willows and cedars stand.
The aroma of donuts
floats through the morning air,
in-between shadows of houses
are sounds of the playground,
listen, hear.

On a park bench
you can find L.P. carved in marker,
yuppies are replaced by youths
when the sky grows darker.
A legendary place
where young people in the city chill,
ball, blaze, drink and pop pills
to get away from the stresses at home.

Kids making out on swings,
"Who got the weed?"
Another cell phone rings.
Hiding beers in barrels
when the cops arrive,
they shine flashlights
in the windows of every ride.
In the summer
teens floss their whips,
step on the gas, bump their systems
and cruise the strip.

A place where neighborhood kids
learn the difference
between good and bad.
You haven't been to Somerville
until you've been down
Lexington Ave.

SELF PORTRAIT

I attempt to draw a portrait of myself without paint or a brush,
I have no skill with some tools, but I am gifted when I grasp a pen full of ink.
I make sure to capture every detail, I try not to rush,
a poem, more effective than a painting, imagine how I look, see how I think.
I sketch, then color, line by line,
leaving behind the shadowy figure which lives inside my mind.

The unfamiliar face covering my insane ideas,
the lookout that houses my telescope like eyes.
My lips, my goatee, my nose and my satellite antenna ears,
my dangerous image covering my heavenly disguise.
A voice the world has not yet heard,
forced to write down everything that occurred.

Working my way down this figure, I come across a treasure buried in my chest.
It contains jewels worth more than anything that could be purchased.
It is the instrument that beat on me to be the best,
its historic fights with sorrow underneath my skin has suddenly surfaced.
The epic battle of good verses evil, sin verses saint,
Lucifer against the Lord, on the ceiling of my belly sketched with paint.

Then there is my back, which carries the world and its weight.
Sometimes it hunches me over and it appears I might fall,
but I will not tip over and crumble, I will keep walking until I am able to stand up straight.
I choose to carry my grief, without it I wouldn't have anything to hold on to at all.
Speaking of holding, I have to mention my hands
which molded life from meaningless strands.

THE BLIND TEACHER

It's the first day of school.
I walk into class,
you see me
and decide I am not going to pass.

Because I am not dressed the same as everyone else
you consider me a problem,
I bet the thought has passed through your head, that if
I was hard up for money, I would
find someone wealthy and rob them.

The year goes on, I pass in work
and never receive a good grade,
you make me feel so dumb,
I want to introduce my wrists to a blade.
If you only took the time to realize
the knowledge I possess,
and with my home life a mess, you only
contribute to the pain in my chest.

I am passing this in to the teacher who is blind.
What you witness is one of a kind,
look beneath my appearance
and I'm sure you'll be surprised what you find!

THE LONG WALK HOME

Forgot how it happened,
the detachment,
finally letting go, escaping the entrapment.

The blades on the skin,
feeling caged in,
running forward without looking behind and waving.

Heart pumping,
feet on the concrete thumping,
running towards uncertainty, running towards something.

Listening to the wind whirl,
ready to hurl,
searching for a new world.

Being alone,
being on your own,
better than living in a broken home.

Heart beats,
hearing whispering from the streets,
cardboard boxes, no more sheets.

Can't escape the rain,
can't escape the pain,
can't escape your brain.

Drugs make you even more lost,
selling your body because you can't afford the cost,
track marks on your arm in the form of a cross.

Harder to clear your mind,

fear that has no concept of time,
clean air makes you blind.

Slowly opening your eyes,
hope is again seen in the skies,
you know the truth because you wrote the lies.

Studying every word,
slowly getting over what occurred,
slowly getting up off the curb.

Realizing your life is a shame,
wondering about the place from where you came,
wondering if it's the same?

Steps backward to move forward,
blessed breaths from the Lord,
back to the place you left, the place where you were first adored.

The day you return
to those who are concerned,
the day your life will turn.

Every addict dreams of this day,
yet to figure out what you will say,
during the long walk home, you vividly remember the way.

I KNEW THIS GIRL FROM DOWNTOWN WHO LIKED TO GET AROUND

I met her in the subway.

It was late at night
as she stepped onto the train
looking for a fight.
Empty, except for a few scattered souls.
She calmed down and asked me for a light.

I told her I was sorry
and that I didn't smoke
as I pulled out the insides of my pockets
to show how badly broke.

I could tell she had been drinking
even though I was sitting
on the opposite side of the train.
Her eyes and mouth
were moving at the speed of light,
but I could tell there was a standstill
inside her brain.

She got up out of her seat
and began to dance around for kicks,
she stood in front of the window
and started to shake her hips.
She grabbed her purse
and put Maybelline on her lashes
and Revlon on her lips.

She finished making herself up,
spun around and stared at me.
Her face, like a book colored by a child

who couldn't stay inside the lines.
Strutted her stuff as she sat down next to me,
whispering in my ear,
asking how she looked countless times.

She removed her jacket
that looked like
a combination of a cape
and a curtain.
Placing her hand on my knee,
I knew for certain
this female was well trained
at the art of flirting.

Attracted to her figure,
but turned off by the way she was acting,
hadn't fallen, but with every action
you could see her concrete skin cracking.

I was focused on shorts
that barely covered her butt,
she wasn't wearing a bra,
only a tight white tank top T-shirt, halfway cut.
Her left nipple served as the period
to the word on her shirt, *SLUT.*

Asked me to come home with her
and mentioned how she liked rough sex.
Battling my emotions,
I declined as I didn't want to take advantage of this girl
with a beautiful body and a clouded mind.

She stepped off the train
and gave me the finger
as the door slammed tight.
I got home, laid in my bed
and turned off the light.

What a night…

LITTLE BIG MAN

Little man, you don't always have to act like a big man.

Little man, don't try to grow up too fast,
you're living through the best times of your life, make them last!
Little man, don't always feel like there is someone you have to impress,
be satisfied with yourself and don't ever second guess.
Little man, you don't always have to look good for the ladies,
trying to appear perfect all the time will end up driving you crazy.

Little man, you don't always have to act like a big man.

Little man, you don't always have to be bad to get in with the cool crowd,
staying silent without being defiant can sometimes speak just as loud.
Little man, don't let the world make you feel so small,
if you have no one to talk to, remember, you can always give me a call.
Little man, don't let others drag you under.
Little man, your little heart is such a small wonder!

Little man, you don't always have to act like a big man.

Little man, don't let mean words upset you,
it's not just a dream, someday people will respect you.
When you feel like you have no strength left, that's when you stay strong.
It doesn't seem like it now, but you will find a place where you belong.
Little man, it's not cool to act dumb and not get good grades,
they'll end up as nobodies and you will march in millions of parades.

Little man, you don't always have to act like a big man.

Little man, there is no one like you in the whole universe,
remember that when things get bad and when things get worse.
Little man, if you're lost for words when they call you a freak,
think for a moment and tell them you're unique!
Little man, you were built with priceless gifts!
Little man, I insist, there is a reason why you exist.

Little man, you don't always have to act like a big man.

LETTER ADDRESSED TO THE DEAD

This letter is sent to spirits
as I search for wisdom
that exists beyond,
this life is not worth living,
I need to know what's next
so I can stay strong and continue on.
I need to know if I will be able to see light
long after my eyes are closed,
I need to know if the soul is the real life
and if the body is just a disguise
that is cleverly covered and clothed.
Will I be able to see my loved ones again
that I miss so much,
will they appear the same and will
I still be able to hear their voice
and feel their loving touch?

Tell me which religion is most righteous,
which religion explains it all
and which religion is most divine?
If I believe in the wrong things
will it hurt my chances
of lasting throughout time?
Could you tell me what God looks like?
Is he black, brown or white?
What does he want from me?
I need to know if it has been Satan
or an unsettled spirit that follows
and continues to haunt me.
Tell me about Hell and tell me about Heaven,
let me know where I will spend the rest of my days.
Explain the secrets of the universe,

like how the sky turns from blue to gray
and who controls the sun and its rays?
Help me to better comprehend space,
it appears to last forever, but does it end?
I'm also interested to know if the wound created by war
between the West and East will be able to mend?
I hope you are not angry with my questions
and I apologize if in any way you have been offended.
I'll be looking forward to a response
once I send it.

Just one more question,
where exactly is your address?
Should I make it out to the dead,
or should I make it out to death?
I'll make sure to leave my location
where you can send your reply.
If you don't have enough time
to answer all of my questions,
just answer the question,
what happens when you die?

BROKEN HEARTS BEAT ON THE COLD CONCRETE

The nameless and the presumed brainless
lifeless on the Lord's ground.
Wind roared, it didn't rain, it poured
as they slept on church stairs
without making a sound.

Broken hearts beat
on the cold concrete.

Wrapped in blankets,
mummies balancing on their tummies
without a pulse.
Crowds of people walked by a situation
they tried to deny.
A sociological scientist reporting my results;
no one helps.

Broken hearts beat
on the cold concrete

Clothes kept close as they wept,
accept, expect to die.
Wanting to perish next
to everything in the world they cherish.
Asking for blessings, silent confessions,
needles, bottle caps and syringes,
signs of lethal injections.

AUTOPSY REPORT (CAUSE OF DEATH)

I received the news he overdosed
and went to visit him
in a hospital bed,
tubes sticking into
every hole in his head.
Skeleton couldn't stop shaking,
couldn't talk, but recognized,
our friendship was something
drugs couldn't even disguise.
Pale skin,
wondering if he would heal.
Father and mother
grateful he survived.

Recovered and released from the hospital,
he tried, but got pried
back with the wrong crowd.
The sound of pleasure, too loud.
An inner struggle
couldn't keep him out of trouble
as he was arrested
for heroine possession.
Suicidal
and drugs contributed to his depression.

Juvenile hall,
scheduled for a stay

from winter to fall.
A record, a release,
on his ankle for six months,
a mechanical leash.

For awhile he stayed away from drugs,
but was still searching for love.
He met a girl at a party who
was heavy into heroine,
she took him back to a place
he had already been.
Under a chemical spell
they became lovers.

Tried to find a way to pay
for his addictions, but couldn't
with a criminal conviction.
Looked for a job, but because of his priors
there was no desire to give him a chance.
Put his worries into the back
of his mind, living blind,
drugs, love,
the ultimate romance.

Received a call from his girl
that would change his world.
He was thinking
about putting their relationship to an end,
her period was late
and she assured him

it was not a mistake.

Wanted to give his child
all he never had.
Former life destructive,
trying to be productive
for the chance to be a dad.

The pressure kept building,
a 19-year-old
who had to worry about raising children.
Trapped with a girl he had no feelings for.
Nowhere to turn for help,
there was only one way
to forever forget.

Alcohol, weed, cocaine, prescription pills,
fully aware this mixture kills.
Overdosed again,
but this time there would be no return.
Pronounced dead on arrival,
there would be no revival.
Rests on his parent's mantel
in an urn.

RHYME AND REASON

Republicans look out for the wealthy, Democrats look out for the poor.
Couldn't we have a party that looked out for every human being
so we wouldn't have to suffer anymore?

The government hides secrets at Area 51.
Don't we have the right to know what exists in space
and hides beyond the sun?

The President declares war and formulates a draft.
Thousands of people die and nothing changes,
add up casualties, subtract blood, times it by tears, do the math.

Every weekend, get drunk and high.
Wake up and contemplate suicide
because you realize the world won't be effected if you live or die.

God bless America, what about God bless the world?
God bless every American little boy
and God bless every Iranian and Iraqi little girl.

Get to work on time every day and see how it pays off.
Work at a company your entire life, a year before you retire
you lose everything and get laid off.

As long as money is more powerful than knowledge criminals will remain at large.
The idea of a man being successful because of his earnings
is society's ultimate mirage.

Kill a madman and create a madder man who will follow.
Save the day,
but make it worse for the children of tomorrow.

My words are filled with facts until the day I leave, man.
In a world full of crime and treason,
my head is filled with rhyme and reason.

SMALL BREASTS

Every morning she checks
the mirror and rubs her eyes.
She turns to the side,
eyes open wide,
checking to see if there is growth
in her bust.
Tears gush down her cheeks
as she stares at a blurred beautiful
reflection in disgust.

In a society
where everything is marketed to teens,
fed images of how she is supposed to look
by movies, TV and magazines.
Having nightmares nobody will like her
instead of having inspiring dreams.

Trying to make them stick out more,
she wiggles and leans,
always wearing an oversized sweatshirt and jeans.

Not thinking about her future,
but of her small fragile frame.
She believes people are more interested with her breasts
then with the meaning of her name.
Wrapped up in a blanket on a Friday night
looking out the window watching it rain,
waiting to hit puberty,
but her time has not yet came.

POINT OF THE GODS

Ones who make the call, creators of all,
blessed with the ability to bounce back.
I have seen these Gods, they do not stand tall,
outsmarting giants, they have quite a knack.
Their wizardry, so silky smooth, so sly.
Crosses and teardrops, suffering a loss,
from coast to coast they are able to fly,
the accuracy of their arched deadly shot.
The backs of their heads are known to have eyes,
known for speeding up and slowing down time.
The heavenly way they float through the skies,
Gods who value the true worth of a dime.
Miracles are performed, everyone stands,
they hold the fate of the globe in their hands.

A JACKET TORN

For days, it didn't move a muscle,
its life had taken a different path.
People hustled by it on their way to work,
lying flat on its back, there it sat.

A dirty color denim
torn to shreds,
dark red stains, flowing veins,
signs that it once had bled.

Existing with its buttons missing,
stitches coming apart at the seams,
A JACKET TORN,
I wonder what it means?
Where are its matching jeans?

Imagine the story this jacket
might have written inside of its pockets?
If only this jacket talked…

Its sleeves were reaching for help,
or they were simply wanting
to remember how skin felt.
The nameless frame which this jacket covered
and the soul which seemed to melt.

This jacket full of holes,
as empty and hollow

as a dreamer's goals.

Taking its new form,
this lifeless jacket, dirty and torn.
Sitting on a concrete wall during a sunny day
or a violent storm.
More than just a piece of clothing
someone use to adorn,
a jacket torn,
by whom was it worn?

II

The roar of gun shots
echoes through the city streets.
No one seems to hear.

LONG SLEEVES

Lisa's father went to fight in a war.
Home alone with her drunken mother, she tried to endure.

She would come home from school and find her mother out cold.
Lisa kept beautiful stories hidden inside, never told.

Pain bottled up, empty bottles swallowed into her mother's hollow gut.
So much sorrow, without anyone in the world to follow, Lisa began to cut.

She changed her wardrobe and began to dress dull.
She didn't want anyone to wonder, she wanted them to know her life was hell.

Her face pale white, clothes as dark as night.
Gore became the color of life.

Every night with a knife she carved into her flesh.
On her knees, skin dripping tears, heavy breath, but not a wish for death.

Stress released with blood.
A ritual Lisa loved.

Never told her best friend, afraid she wouldn't understand the blade's feel.
It was about the hurt, but Lisa also loved watching it heal.

Sometimes Lisa would slice her skin under the stars
as the moon illuminated new blood and old scars.

Morbid memories of pain in the past.
Cut through high school and wore long sleeves to class.

No one bothered to ask, so Lisa never bothered to speak.
GOTHIC FREAK.

Time lines on her arms telling a gory tale.
Lisa will wear long sleeves until her heart heals.

Blood rolls, look, there it goes! A cover up with clothes.
Long sleeves, shadowing secret scabs that continue to grow.

FOOTPRINT

It’s winter now and the world is frozen.
Icicles remind me of tears unable to fall to the ground.
Peers who had their fate chosen, the gates to Heaven are quickly closing,
the echo of fallen friends makes a stirring sound.
Shovel out sorrow and make a path for joy,
things come into focus as we grow older,
back to innocence as a little girl or boy,
my heart grows colder.
Rushing out the door, on my way,
equipped with all my belongings, I don’t know how long I’ll be,
no one wants to listen, I have nothing left to say,
traveling through a blizzard, I can barely see.
A footprint left in the snow,
follow its path, it will show you where to go.

DEAD MAN'S PROMISE

Skulls and bones wearing crowns sitting on thrones,
fleshless fingers wrapped around instruments that help spirits speak.
Trapped in a wicked wasteland and aimlessly roams
among the weak and obsolete.

A heart has 10 beats left before it finally stops,
the sound of sacrifice, silent as the stoppage of the world's clocks.
For years this body has had a scent similar to when a corpse rots,
candlelight vigils held on different streets and blocks.

Don't be surprised that after this demise to witness them rise,
not even death allows a peaceful rest.
After darkness, witness opening eyes,
put your ear on their tombstone to hear a fluttering chest.

An empty casket still sealed tight, where did they go?
Dead man missing, stay quiet and listen to the sound.
Look deep into your hearts and all of you will know,
this is one dead man who couldn't be kept in the ground.

Dead man arrives and survives by traveling through air,
when you see this dead man, don't be filled with fear.
Waiting for this dead man to once again reappear,
dead men keep their promises, I swear.

STRONG SHOULDERS

I admire the way you handle
the problems you are dealt,
the average person who received as much pain
would crumble and melt.
I can see it in your eyes,
your stress,
you walk proudly
not letting anyone know you are truly a mess.
Amazed, yet bewildered,
at how you can keep going,
so much sorrow in your sight
without letting anyone know.

Unbelievable
how you live,
things have been taken from you your entire life,
you do nothing, but give.
I think I figured out
why you are quick to help,
finding a way to dismiss
the hurt you've felt.
A human being assembled to carry
the heaviest of boulders,
that is why you will always find my worried head
resting on your shoulders.

DANCING GOLDEN TEARS

Elisa was 15-years-old
with a beautiful face.
When she cried, dripping down her cheek, dancing tears made of gold.
Tried her best, did all she could,
her family still greeted her with stares so cold.
Elisa felt worthless, no good.

Not allowed to express herself,
Elisa begged to be understood.
Mom picked her outfits, controlling everything that sat on the shelf.
Verbally and physically abused during her adolescence,
no one to talk to, no one to tell she needed help.
Elisa was never able to express the true emotions of her essence.

Eventually, Elisa ran out of things to say.
Prayed and asked God for his blessings
as she planned her escape, it felt like the only way.
All her life she dreamed to be a dancer.
An entire family ridiculed
the meaning of her life. Elisa was desperately looking for an answer.

Elisa packed her dancing shoes in a bag and decided to jet,
leaving behind a note explaining the reason for her escape in a small stanza.
Upset, she cried until sentences on the paper were soaking wet.
Elisa leaped out her bedroom window and ran after a dream,
catching her breath, she stopped and stared into a sunset.
A love for dancing, many cannot understand what that means.

Left her family knowing
her soul might come apart at the seams,
Elisa never looked back, she kept going.
Elisa took a chance,
into a famous dancer she kept growing.
Her star now shines bright under the darkness of staged night. Elisa will forever dance.

A FINAL KISS GOODBYE

This kiss is blown

to everyone who ever loved and admired me
and it's blown to those who were never too fond.
It's for those who didn't fall in love with my fame and fortune,
this kiss is placed on the face of those who loved me all along.
This kiss is for the woman who was meant to hold my hand
and walk with me on my wedding day down the aisle.
This kiss is placed on the face
of the only girl in the whole world who could make me smile.
This kiss is blown to those who looked out for my best interests,
it's for those who never took advantage of me, so the number is few.
As you read this, it could be very likely,
that this final kiss goodbye was meant, just for you.

This kiss is blown

to everyone who believed and trusted in me
with all their heart.
This kiss is placed on the face of those who knew
the light inside of me would shine in the deepest of dark.
This kiss is blown to all those who never met me
and it's for all those who knew me extremely well.
This kiss is placed on the face of everyone
who was aware I lived each day halfway between Heaven and Hell.
This kiss is blown to the world, my time on earth is coming to an end.
When I leave, you might miss me, but try not to cry,
blown from my loving lifeless lips,
I send to you

a final kiss goodbye.

MEN'S ROOM

Greetings, from a daily gathering of gentlemen
who conduct morning meetings underneath towers of dusty books.
A perverse palace of pestilence to tidy up looks,
paved under permanent dirt is potential which lived way back when.
As you float through the door, feet fasten to the floor.
Above toilet gates are clouds which will not dissipate, like fog on a stagnant summer shore.
Shaving in the sink, bathing un-bashfully without a blink, the rigorous resentful trend.
Tobacco wrapped white wet leaves, foliage which won't flush in puddles of urine.
Sketched on stench soaked stalls are senile sermons,
tales of denial someone felt they had to mention.
Mirrors are purposely painted with filth so no one can see their reflection,
no one wants to be reminded of what is, what was and what might have been.
The little bit of life left lingering in a vagrant's valiant veins,
in the Boston Public Library, a scene in the everyday life of homeless men.
Stains and the shame of unknown names is all that remains.

BYE, NIGHT.

Bye, night.
Morning's light illuminate's pain
as yellow tape cautioned where not to step.
Plastic rope, strangled hope,
where the young man took his final breath.

12:59 A.M.
the estimated time his soul was slain.
If only the sidewalk outlined in chalk could talk,
it would tell of the murderer
who lived up the block.
A spirit screaming for help, help which never came.
His black hat walking down the street as the wind blows,
the spot where he was violently killed,
every day his mother goes, to bring
flowers, candles and pictures of her son.
She breaks down and cries under these city skies
thinking about what he might have become.

The wind is still.
Grow up, he never will.
This is the day a gun roared
over the voice of the Lord.
A short lived life
too often ignored.

A FEAST WITH THE DECEASED

Ghosts gathering by a table eager to eat, figures that float and no longer walk on feet.
A supernatural last supper full of ghouls and goblins,
a spiritual situation, over dinner the dead discuss their damnation.
Those plagued with paranormal problems.
This is a feast with the deceased,
raise your glass to those who passed and give a ghostly toast, REST IN PEACE.

The air exclusively eerie, the scenery so scary.
As food floats, you can see it funnel down transparent throats,
as the dead break bread,
these horrid hosts, these grim gruesome ghosts.
This is a feast with the deceased,
raise your glass to those who passed and give a ghostly toast, REST IN PEACE.

The setting, unearthly upsetting,
on cemetery dirt they dine.
A graveyard feast for those who can never rest in peace,
they raise their glasses of wine dripping with slime.
This is a feast with the deceased,
raise your glass to those who passed and give a ghostly toast, REST IN PEACE.

Eating flesh from bones while sitting in thrones shaped like tombstones,
hearing moans as they munch, gauntly grieving.
Eating off plates inscribed with dreadful dates,
meditating on their mysterious meaning.
This is a feast with the deceased,
raise your glass to those who passed and give a ghostly toast, REST IN PEACE.

Dwelling over dessert, those who hopelessly hurt.
Bits of bodies baked into a cobweb cream cake,
they cannot blow out the candles flame until they are reincarnated with a new name,

fatally frosted with their future fate.
This is a feast with the deceased,
raise your glass to those who passed and give a ghostly toast, REST IN PEACE.

Dinner has ended, in the air these lost souls suspended.
Every moment is their last meal
and just like they were never here, these demons deceptively disappear.
Creatures without a care vanishing into the midnight air, these spirits set sail.
This is a feast with the deceased,
raise your glass to those who passed and give a ghostly toast, REST IN PEACE.

A BEAUTIFUL ROSE

Even though we hear cries,
remember, this is a beautiful rose
that never dies,
this is a beautiful rose that forever grows.

I look out there and stare
at all of you today,
each and everyone of you is wearing a sad face.
We wish we could see this beautiful rose walk
down the aisle, but we have to believe
this flower blooms in a better place.

There is nothing to be depressed about,
this beautiful rose
lived a long and lovely life,
and today it has come to an end.
Remember, even though this beautiful rose is gone,
she will always be my grandmother,
your mother, your aunt, our friend.

No person has had more of an impact on my life
and I bet many of you can say the same,
her body will leave the world we live in,
her presence, her power, her beauty
and her spirit will remain.

I do not see doom, depression,
disgust and despair,
when I think of my grandmother
I think of a beautiful rose
surrounded by white doves
gliding gracefully through the air.

This beautiful rose was tired and worn out

from taking care of us and holding our hands,
both yours and mine.
Let us follow the footsteps
this beautiful rose left behind
that are forever trapped in the sands of time.

She never once put herself first,
it was always about me and you.
Let us think for a moment,
isn't that something
we should all work on and try to do?

A beautiful rose that was one of
the most beautiful people
to ever walk this earth and bless us with her grace,
this beautiful rose, we will never forget its shape,
we will never forget its face.

All of you, wipe those tears off of your cheek!
My grandmother wouldn't want that,
please, there is no reason to cry,
the more we celebrate her life and her ways,
the more this beautiful rose will never die!

Let us show God,
that a beautiful rose is what has been taken.
Even though our hearts are breaking,
let us not be mistaken,
let us show this beautiful rose our appreciation
and make the angels awaken!
Let us break this silence
and give this beautiful rose what she deserves,
let us give her a standing ovation!

Even though right now all we hear is cries,
remember, this is a beautiful rose
that never dies,
this is a beautiful rose that forever grows.

SITTING ON THE STAIRWAY TO SALVATION

Walking on my way to work
I saw a woman sitting on church stairs,
her palms tightly pressed together looking up
towards the heavens, moving her lips lightning quick saying prayers.
She never believed in God, but found herself sitting on his stairs.
Started to believe in a higher power
after figuring out no one down here cares.
I was far away, but I was well aware of what made
her hair gray, I felt her deepest darkest fears.
From where I was standing I heard her sighing, she started crying,
shedding troublesome tears all over those holy stairs.

She was heavily breathing
and wanted with all of her heart
to begin believing.
She was sitting on the stairway to salvation
praying to possess a stress free soul
that wouldn't give into this earth's temptation.

Sitting on the stairs shaking, hoping to awaken
from a deep dark dream that couldn't seem more real.
A lost soul looking to take control of her meaningless life,
I thought to myself and said, "That's the exact same way I feel."
I could see the pain on her face and imagined how her insides looked,
mumbling a prayer to once and for all heal,
she was running out of time

and was searching desperately for the Holy Grail.
A journey to the afterlife is long, we wish for someone to watch
over us when it is time to set sail.

I thought about what life does to people,
I pray not to grow up and be in the same position,
how horrible it would be to live through every day of your life
and feel like there is something missing.
I'm sure she has sat on the stairway to salvation before
and got up quickly after realizing God didn't even have time to listen.
She had on dirty clothes that could never be cleansed, I wonder
if this woman ever had a chance to glisten?
She sat on the stairway to salvation like all of us will at some point,
trying to find a reason to continue existing.

She was heavily breathing
and wanted with all of her heart
to begin believing.
She was sitting on the stairway to salvation
praying to possess a stress free soul
that wouldn't give into this earth's temptation.

Whether or not our purpose ever rises to the surface,
or maybe it will stay buried underneath all of our desire?
Trying to please everyone of our bodily needs won't bring us up
towards the clouds, but down towards the fire.
I am an angel waiting in the wings here on earth wondering
if I'm holy enough for God to hire,
my spirit is turning sour
and is ready to expire.
I found myself sitting next to this woman on the stairway to Heaven,
we both hoped to sit somewhere higher.

I LIVE IN A FAR AWAY PLACE

I'll never forget
the way they rushed in
and intruded my space.
That's why I live
in my far away place.

I'll never reveal
the place where I hide,
my far away place where I reside.
It's a place
where I don't have to be alarmed,
those who harmed me, I will never have to fear.
I got in my car and drove,
kept my foot on the gas
not knowing which way to steer.

Disappearing
in my rearview mirror, the city streets
which kept me walking in a maze.
Finally, on my skin, the long arms of the sun's rays.

I have been on the move
for many days.
Not looking for my new home, my new home will find me.
A peaceful paradise
where beauty will blind me.

The sadness, there is none in my far away place
which will remind me.
A fresh start, a new heart.
When I first seen it, never would have been able to dream it,
coming from inside, the strumming of harps.

I arrived
just as it was turning dark.
I saw a blue jay sitting on a stone.
I live in a far away place
and it is the first time in my life I feel like I am home.

LONELY GIRL LOOKING OUT THE WINDOW LISTENING TO THE WIND BLOW

Lonely girl looking out a window listening to the wind blow.
Sees her ghostly reflection as she stares,
gazing for hours hoping, wishing
to find something, someone that cares.
She sees a transparent image
of her own troublesome tears.

Lonely girl looking out a window listening to the wind blow.
Standing with frail fingers on her hips,
wondering if she will find the love of her life
that will change her world with a kiss on the lips.
Searching desperately for a reason to remain,
a reason to exist.

Lonely girl looking out a window listening to the wind blow.
The window gets foggy from hopeless breaths blown from her nose,
standing there for hours wondering
why she was not chose.
Looking like a statue
in a perfectly painful sculpted pose.

Lonely girl looking out a window listening to the wind blow.
She puts her fingers up to the fog and draws a heart
which is illuminated by streetlights
pulsating in the dark.
She had so many plans for the future,
but never quite knew where to start.

Lonely girl looking out a window listening to the wind blow.
She stares with blurred vision,
nowhere to go,
her room is a prison.
Lonely girl looking out a window, wondering why she is still living?
She begs for the world to see her, but for now
she pulls down the shade, wanting to remain hidden.

A DAMSEL IN DISTRESS NAMED DANIELLE

Danielle's summer
was hot as hell,
had a summer reading list,
but she wasn't too concerned
about trying to read and trying to spell.
Only 15, but had seen
that wearing tight tops
attracted the most handsome looking
sexy, spectacular, sculpted jocks.
Her sultry style got her a date
with the schools biggest stud,
he arrived at her parent's house looking spiffy,
he brought flowers and even
greeted her mom with a hug.
Sometimes the sweetest looking face
covers up a soul that is bitter,
pulled into an empty parking lot,
didn't waste any time trying to flirt,
he just lifted up her skirt and did her.

At school her story
was being discussed by groups of girls near lockers,
everyone was shocked Danielle
and this model of a looking man hooked up,
it was one of the semesters biggest shockers.
The gorgeous guy walked down the hallway confidently
with an extra small tight white T-shirt
and a pair of Dockers.
Overnight, Danielle went from a nobody
to becoming a goddess at her school,
no one wanted to take her to a dance

or give her a glance, nothing but a feminine fool.
Now, she makes penis' pulsate inside of boys pants,
they stare and drool.
Danielle's confidence grew
and there was not a thing anyone could do,
she started sleeping around
and became the high school whore,
her dreams were coming true…
Always in detention,
a great way to get a boy's attention,
she was the girl everyone knew.

Danielle was a good student, but once she
started stripping and skipping, down dropped
her draws and her grades.
Started coming to class thinking she was a star,
rocking beautiful braids and dark shades
and every speckle of glitter on her body
stood for all the people who she laid.
On the outside Danielle couldn't be more happy,
on the inside, she couldn't be more afraid.
Went to the clinic and got tested for AIDS,
tested positive,
astonished and amazed.
Contracted HIV and
Danielle isn't sure if she will make it to age 23,
everything she wanted ruined her
and now Danielle dreams
of everything she used to be.

It wasn't too long ago,
Danielle was a good girl,
now she carries around her filth
and everywhere she goes

she carries her guilt.
Every skimpy outfit
she threw out and said, “Good riddance!”
She cries when she sees the same boys and knows
they will only touch her
if they are wearing mittens.
Danielle is just one of many girls
who tries to be with the in-crowd,
all those girls who walk in Danielle’s high heel shoes,
just be real, I hope you are hearing
Danielle’s story clearly and loud.
If Danielle’s life could help change another
she would be proud.

Danielle is a damsel in distress,
I don’t have to ramble any longer,
you know Danielle’s life is a mess.
She awaits her sentence of death
and leaves her house everyday
wearing a long black dress.

GOD BLESS......

UNKNOWN LOVERS IN THE NEVADA NIGHT

The mysterious shapes of the numbers intrigued me deeply,
I was drawn in by the unknown.
Wrestling back and forth with the decision
as every organ in my body became overgrown.
I lifted up the phone and heard the loneliness of the tone,
it hung up in the air, almost to my ear, until I silenced the noise.
My fingers and hands were trembling, sweat stagnant on my brow,
this was going to be a night where I would be, one of the boys.
For long enough the decision swayed, the call was made.
In my mind the scenario continued to dangle
as I mentally explored it from every angle.
Lured by the curves of phone numbers,
someone had their hands around my conscience and started to strangle.

Alone in a hotel room in Vegas, my tools tarnished with rust.
10:29 and the moment was mine, I heard thumps of weightless feet,
my blood began to rush, hush… fingers massaging the door as
I gently opened, palms soaking from who I did greet.
In the stillness of the Nevada night I witnessed a breathtaking sight.
Shook hands, skin warmer than desert sand,
for years I swore off any personal pleasure,
but for this one moment, I would remember how it felt to be a man.
In this Vegas dream, her skin caramel cream,
she undressed as I sat on the corner of the bed and gazed.
She strutted towards me, skin without waves,
pushing softly on my shoulder blades, her fingers grazed.
Touching every strand trying to find the man in me,
I stared into the eyes of an unknown strangers perfection.
Grabbing onto what holds the juices of life
and just like the Vegas strip, things began to move in an up and down direction.
Half of her body on top of mine, hands caressing my body like a pen does a line,
completely shut down, the wisdom which lives in my mind.
I searched her body looking for something I knew I would not find,
the lights of Las Vegas flickering and flashing, our oiled bodies shine.
Whether this moment meant anything to either one of us
is still undiscovered,
as my plane hovers,
the tale of two unknown lovers.

III

My neighborhood friends
disappeared off this earth. Now
I chill with tombstones.

TELL ME WHAT THE DAY WAS LIKE

Could someone please tell me what the day was like?
Tell me if the sky mirrored the ocean's reflection,
tell me if it was one of those days
when the sun shined in every direction with precise perfection?

Could someone please tell me what the day was like?
Tell me if it was one of those days when leaves stood still,
tell me if it was one of those days
when you could leave your house without a jacket and not feel a chill?

Could someone please tell me what the day was like?
Tell me if it was one of those days when sidewalks sparkled like diamonds,
tell me if it was one of those days
when you went to sleep under a summer moonlight shining?

Could someone please tell me what the day was like?
Tell me if it was one of those days when parks were filled with joy,
tell me if it was one of those days
that brings out smiles on the faces of little girls and boys?

Could someone please tell me what the day was like?
Tell me if it was one of those days when you wished there was a 25th hour,
could someone please tell me what the day was like
when you come to my grave and place a flower?

PREGNANCY'S TRIGGER

Amy wants to be all she can be,
society won't let her.
Confidence diminishing, she wants to feel better.
Has to make a decision,
with no one to listen, she decides alone.
Rushes to a party where she gets high
and taken advantage of by a mysterious guy.

Months later her stomach
is stretched out and swollen,
rolling down a corridor, her water has broken.
During the pregnancy
there was plenty of drinking and smoking.
The baby was born at a dangerous birth weight.
Amy is hoping it will heal, trying to deal,
the father in jail, however,

he recently signed a waiver
to get out on good behavior.
Spent months dreaming of seeing his little girl,
wanted to return as the savior.
Wasn't ready to meet the man
taking his place, it shattered his world.
Snapped, went on a war path,
wanted everyone to feel his wrath.
Thinking of the other man made him want to hurl.
Beyond mentally ill, at the point

where he could kill.

22 is his age,
veins circulating rage.
His only reason for living is revenge,
like an animal let out of a cage, starving.
Encouraged to do the deed by convict friends, bred
with the type of heart that never mends.
Just got out of the pen, has no problem going back in,
being behind steel bars is better than having to feel.

The day has come.
Pictures his daughter
while staring down the barrel of a gun,
imagining the slaughter.
He drives to their house and parks by the curb,
making sure he's not heard.
Approaches the house, kicks down the door
and squeezes.

SOUND OF THE PLAYGROUND

Swinging stickball bats and basketballs dribbling,
kids with chalk on the ground scribbling while birds are singing,
kids hanging around diddling.

A slap shot, a football being caught,
today no one has fought.
When you're young, the playground is the spot.

Kick balls whipped,
chips eaten, sodas sipped,
sneakers scrape the ground from a hop scotch skip.

Kids running around playing tag,
kids glow as they boast and brag,
snacks someone brings back from the store in a plastic bag.

Wheels on bikes spinning,
excitement, a new day at the playground is beginning,
kids wanting a chance at winning, begging to play one more inning.

Kids running through sprinklers, clothes soaking wet,
at the playground no one is ever upset,
kids getting tired, sitting back and watching the sun set.

Frisbees flying,
a kid who has to go home begins crying,
who ever said, "Heaven is a playground," sure wasn't lying.

FOREST OF SOMBER

Lost
for quite sometime inside
this forest of somber.
Left to ponder.
Left to wander.

This forest
once pulsated with life,
but the trees, the leaves and the animals
all started to die.

I know my chances
are slim
as I step over dead branches
limb by limb.

I wish to exit,
the way out, I don't know
where to begin.
Time crawls
in the forest of somber
as I touch my face and notice
the wrinkles under my chin.

The forest of somber
rarely gets rain,
except from sprinkles of sin
that shower its skin.

In the cold and bitter dark
I rest my back upon some bark.

I will ponder

until I find enough energy to wander.
Chances of my survival
are becoming weaker,
chances of my demise
are becoming stronger.
I dwell
in the forest of somber.

AUDREY'S ASSAULT

The family secret remains hidden, an act unspeakable, unforgiving.
Audrey keeps it concealed within her frivolous frame,
the hurt cannot be healed until it's revealed, no one to trust, the truth of her father's lust.
Once she was violated her worth was never the same, imagine the thoughts in her brain.
A father ignored the plea, "Halt!"
Forced to keep emotions locked inside her heart's vault,
it's not her fault,
this is Audrey's assault.

It started before she reached her teens, the father entering his dreams through her jeans.
Explained how no one would listen to her screams, still not quite sure what it means.
Audrey accepts what she has been given, started to believe this was a normal way of living.
The experience ends, left in the corner looking out the window at the moon's gleam.
A father ignored the plea, "Halt!"
Forced to keep emotions locked inside her heart's vault,
it's not her fault,
this is Audrey's assault.

Told a friend about their romance, father saying, "I love you," while pulling down her pants.
Best friend told her, "When you get a chance, find someone to tell."
Audrey extremely nervous, her friend saying, "You don't deserve this!"
Seduced by his sexual spell, the way he would yell, the way he would make her face swell.
A father ignored the plea, "Halt!"
Forced to keep emotions locked inside her heart's vault,
it's not her fault,

this is Audrey's assault.

As she got a little older, became tired of the lynching way he used to hold her.
Wished she could cure her mother's cancer in order to find the answer she needed.
Went through this by herself, all day lying to herself, at night never lying by herself.
Leaving for school everyday feeling defeated, depressed, drained, depleted.
A father ignored the plea, "Halt!"
Forced to keep emotions locked inside her heart's vault,
it's not her fault,
this is Audrey's assault.

In a private journal she described how her father entered inside.
The internal pain she felt, when touched, her skin would melt.
Mom terminally ill, father overpowering her with his will, "Stay still!"
An image never to leave the mind, the way a father unbuckled his belt.
A father ignored the plea, "Halt!"
Forced to keep emotions locked inside her heart's vault,
it's not her fault,
this is Audrey's assault.

ALONE FOREVER

Constantly searching for a companion, I
don’t see the point.
When a loved one leaves your heart, you
feel the pain in every joint.
If I eventually find someone to say, “I do,”
the happiness won’t last for long because
caskets are built for one, not two.

KEVIN THE CAN MAN

I would see this man every morning at the same time,
he was always pushing his carriage full of cans.
Most would think he lived a meaningless life,
but I could tell, that in his mind, he still had gigantic plans.
One day I worked up enough courage
and introduced myself to him,
he stared back at me with an unshaven face,
a scar over his lip and dirt under his chin.

"Cans, cans,
are there any in that barrel over there?"

"I'm not sure," I replied.
"If there are, I am not aware."

"Ok thanks," said the man.
"I will see you around."

"Hold on," I said.
"Every morning I see you
and I hear that sound,
the sound of the cans
in the carriage you push."

He fired back, "I'm not going to give you
any of my cans, is this some sort of ambush?"

"No, no," I replied.
"I just wanted to say you are someone I admire."

"Me?" said the man shocked. "Most people think I am
just some bum who no longer has any ambition or desire."
"Because I don't wear the nicest clothes

and because they think this is the profession I chose."

"This was not my dream,
but sometimes that is just how life goes."

He said this while wiping the snots on his sleeve
that were dripping from his nose,
this revealed his T-shirt
covered with blood and holes.

"This was not the life I always dreamed of
I too, was a part of this society and I still have lofty goals."

I stared into his eyes and saw a glimmer
that still glowed off his dirty face.
He showed me a photo of a huge house and said,

"This was once my place.
I used to live the life everyone dreamed of,
but that was before my tragic fall from grace.
I always planned carefully on how not to lose my fortune,
but I never prepared on how not to lose my mind."

"Then one day it happened,
and it was like I was living in a new world, a new time.
In my minds eye I tried to think back on all that made me happy,
but I was totally blind.
Now I stay drunk all day
so I don't have to remember
how I lost everything two years ago

on the 21st day of December.
I had a wife, but we weren't able to have children,
she was my life.
She got liver cancer and died quickly,
and all of a sudden I was a husband without a wife,
a man without a plan.
a man that was suddenly all alone."

"I stopped going to work
and I made these streets my home.
So, my new job is
collecting cans from nine to five,
that's how I eat
and how I stay alive.
I am going to save up enough money from these cans
to rebuild my life, find a new wife and start over,
I will stop this drinking
and once again be able to live sober!
The shock of what happened to me
is all part of the past,
I just hope I am going to be able to continue
and not run out of gas.
This money I get from these cans, I can't tell you where,
but I hide it all in a secret little stash."

He clutched onto the bar of his carriage
and started racing,
I never looked at homeless people the same
after Kevin and I had a conversation.

DISCIPLINE AND WISDOM

The search for infinite wisdom,
to achieve great knowledge
all you have to do is open your ears and listen.

What makes a person smart
has nothing to do with how much you know,
over time, the way to achieve wisdom
has become a lost art.

Discipline
is the key that opens doors,
food,
objects we consume,
if the diet we digest daily
doesn't go down smooth, it can bring us to our doom.

It's better to have an empty stomach
than to have a stomach that is always full,
years of sitting down at the table
and having been fed bull.

When your stomach is empty
you search for more,
when your stomach is full
you lie down and snore.

If you're always satisfied
you'll never know what it's like to starve,
just like a person who has never been deeply hurt,
will never know how it feels to be scarred.

Don't let your stomach and your head get too fat,

be weary of what you eat.
Believing you always deserve something,
you are quick to serve yourself a treat.
Don't eat too much that is sweet
and watch as your mindset carries over to everyday life,
watching closely where you place your feet.

Foods high in saturated fat clog arteries
and clutter veins with grease,
your stomach and your mind
will never be at peace.

This applies to everything in life
as circumstances get more complex,
pleasure and satisfaction
yes, I'm talking about sex.
From the top to the bottom,
going down and staying above,
being with too many people over a period of time
makes you forget how to use your heart,
you forget how to love.

Now you are gaining experience
and superior knowledge,
how to act as a person
is a class they do not teach in college.
The real education
on how to control virtue and vice.
Discipline
has brought you
wisdom,
bringing you
perfect vision.
Take care of yourself
and gain compassion for other people's hearts,
they can claim to know it all,
but in my book,
this is what I call being smart.

WHITHER AWAY

Frozen in time while I impose the rhyme,
I've chosen to dine with the dead,
finally closing my mind.
Leaves blow blustery around my body's frame,
please trust in my name,
rust covers the man who was slain.

The night sky is gloomy,
no longer does it consume me,
wondering when I might die?
The inalienable right to say goodbye as
I let out a light cry.
I pray the God's protect me
and inject me with afterlife,
for me there is no other destiny,
look how little there is left of me!

Nothing left but bones,
nothing left that I own,
stillness, silence, moans,
sleeping on a tombstone
being eaten away by crows,
skeleton covered by clothes,
in each hand, a pen and a rose.

Times are tragic, a man made of magic,
mental perception of a picture
that couldn't be more graphic.
Snakes and worms cover my corpse,
they slither where I lay,
overhead the sky is bitter and gray,
death is delivered on this day,
I begin to whither away.

LETTER TO SOMEONE WHO IS THINKING ABOUT TAKING THEIR LIFE

Dear Friend,

The sun shines during the day
and the moon glows during the night,
during these times you feel
something just isn't right.

You are special
and so is your life.

There isn't anything good in your world,
trust me, I know exactly how you feel.
You and I both wake up every morning rubbing our eyes
because the world we call ours
doesn't seem real.

I know that's why you cheat
and why you steal,
if love entered your body
a broken heart would magically heal.

I have to go now and I know you too
are thinking about exiting this earth
because you believe no one would shed any tears,
I want you to remember this letter
when you feel like nobody cares.

P.S.

I hope to see you soon,
I wait eagerly for your reply.
You might feel all alone, but I want you to know
if anything ever happened to you,
I am someone who would acknowledge your life,
I am someone who would cry.

BIRTH OF A BUTTERFLY UNDERNEATH A BRIDGE

The mammoth shadow of a city bridge
standing up on its giant dirty legs.
Covering all which mysteriously lives,
the homeless sleeping on their concrete cribs.
Darkness is avoided, the silence begs,
a caterpillar crawls inside steel walls.
Dancing desperately with death and decay,
getting pushed around by violent squalls.
The sound crashing on the ground when night falls,
lacking knowledge to fly into the fray.
Crunched in a cocoon, it's time will come soon.
Adorned with armor, waiting to be reborn
under the magical mist of the moon.
The birth, twilights transformational tune
and the shape of its breathtaking new form.
No one taught the butterfly how to soar,
it learned of its special gifts on its own.
It built up enough courage to explore,
now part of the world's beautiful décor.

PERFECTLY WRITTEN STORY

I am not quite sure how it started.
I am not quite sure how it will end.

I dream about living a happy life,
I wake up and realize it was pretend.
I am coming into the middle of the book
and have yet to make a decision on whether it is good or bad,
a few days might be joyful,
but the majority remain sad.
Rushing to the end of the page,
what comes next has to be better!
I would have never began
if I knew the entire novel would consist of bad weather!
People are afraid to pick up a copy
because the cover looks too complicated to figure out,
if they would just open it up and look inside, it would
no longer be a mystery to what it is I'm about.
Begging for someone
to read the first chapter, then
maybe I could have a day
where I experienced a little laughter.

We know the beginning and the middle do not matter
as long as the end is filled with glory,
that would be the conclusion
to my perfectly written story.

IV

She is sniffing lines.
I am writing lines. Will we
find what we search for?

THE SMARTEST MAN I NEVER MET

The man snuck into a library
where he secretly lived for months.
I was given orders by my boss
to clean out his room,
I did, but my curiosity
also made me rummage
through his backpack.
It seemed as though every possession
the man owned was in this bag,
little trinkets which told stories
about his past.

The homeless man
was a chemical biologist
who spoke five languages
and was outstanding at math.
He was a college graduate who attended
Harvard and M.I.T.
I began to wonder how a brilliant man
could end up living up in a 10-foot-wide closet?

I continued to search through his bag.
I found health magazines,
I also found a few *Playboys* and a bottle of lotion,
along with a large poster
of a beautiful beach showing the sun
reflecting off the ocean.

His green jacket hung over the chair,
it smelled like a mixture

of urine, sperm, crumbs and grease,
stains on his jacket covered stains on his soul,
I wondered about long nights
and if there was any peace?

I wished I could have spoken to him
to find out what made him so upset,
my hello and goodbye
to the smartest man I never met.

AS THE NIGHT GOES ON

As the night goes on
I think about who has taught me
right from wrong.
Her smile glows
with a light so strong,
my mom.

My mom has a heart
made out of gold.
Mom, forgive me
for not always doing
what I was told.

We don't appreciate our moms
until we get a little wiser
and a little older.
My mom never had a place to go
when she was sad,
but she was the first to let you cry
on her shoulder.

As the night goes on
all I can think about is the life of my mom.
I wish I could hold her,
I could never pay her back
all that I owe her.

My mom has been picked on a lot
because she was caring,
she lived a life that was so daring,
my mom was all about sharing.

Even when she was sick,

she would still be a mother,
as the night goes on
all I can think about is my mom
and how she is like no other.

When I was sick
she would treat me like a king,
whether it be day or night,
anything I asked for,
she would get me anything.
Always made sure I was healthy,
her main reason for living
was to help me.
She would call me
to make sure I was ok,
it was an ordinary day
for my mom to go out of her way.

I am her only son
and she is my only mom,
I'll never be able to thank her enough
for all she has done.

When people in my family fought
my mom was the first to bring them back together,
as the night goes on
all I can do is think about my mom,
throughout my life I'll remember her ways forever.

I write this to you as a man,
I have my mom to thank
for all that I have and all that I am.

Mom, I hope you understand

how much I see you as a hero,
I'm far away from you now
as I stare at your picture on my bureau.
No matter how far away I am,
in my heart I will always save a place,
throughout my life
I'll never forget your special face.

As the night goes on
I think about who has taught me
right from wrong.
Her smile glows
with a light so strong,
my mom.

CLOSE YOUR EYES AND DREAM WITH ME

Close your eyes and dream with me
and imagine everything you ever wanted to be,
after long enough of mentally viewing your deepest desires,
you will live inside the fantasy you used to just see.

Close your eyes and dream with me
and imagine peace in your heart and peace in your mind,
suffering is a stage we must all experience,
it will not last forever throughout time.

Close your eyes and dream with me
and imagine holding everything out of your grasps,
you outsmarted your enemies and now you rule the world
and there's no reason why your reign can't forever last.

Close your eyes and dream with me
and let's block out everything that distracts us,
sin makes us feel better immediately,
that's the reason it attracts us.

Close your eyes and dream with me
and imagine changing all that is wrong,
dream about building a peaceful place
where us outcasts finally feel like we belong.

Close your eyes and dream with me
and imagine all the problems, poverty and pain disappearing,
dream about living inside a world

where everyone's characters were created for caring.

Close your eyes and dream with me
and imagine loving everything you once hated,
fulfilling your ultimate destiny,
the reason why you were created.

Close your eyes and dream with me
go ahead and shut them tight,
and continue to dream that everyone will view the world
and see the same beautiful sight.

THE PERFECT PRESENT

It sat under a tree, a present no one bothered to see.
It was the holiday season and for some reason, this gift was not perfectly wrapped.
Its' ribbon was torn, bent and broken, the present did not take on a beautiful form.
It wasn't decorated with holiday hues, no reds, no greens, the present was solid black.

Kids swiped pretty presents away, the ugly present was left to stay,
lingering until it was the only present left.
Under a beautiful tree's gleam was the portrait of a present that looked so mean.
No one realized it contained one of the greatest secrets ever kept.

The lights on the tree dimmed, gone was the glow of the last child's grin,
he believed the best gifts were taken.
What was on his wish list, in this little beaten up box could never exist.
Boy was he mistaken!

The gorgeous gifts were gone, a lonely child stood wondering what went wrong?
A Christmas song disappeared as the child looked to the heavens and stared.
He undid the ribbon, opening the only present which was never given.
He cheered! Amazed at what appeared!

A little dark box that when opened showed the world's light, it changed the boy's life.
The lonely child and the lonely present now share a special bond.
What was in the box? Never to tell the secret, so special a gift, the child will forever keep it.
A present that will last long after another Christmas has come and gone.

This peculiar looking present is patient, wrapped up and waiting
for all of us to find.
We must look past the nonsense if we wish to see its wonderful contents
and open the perfect present everyone else has left behind.

ROSARY BEADS THAT BLEED

The life I lost, the divine sign of the cross.
In the name of the Father, Son and the Holy Spirit, Amen,
the pointless pain of slain men,
blood pours out of my pen.

Hands tightly together squeezed while on my knees with rosary beads that bleed,
listen to lightning strike as I recite the apostles creed.

Our Father let my art make it to heaven so my brethren know where they're heading,
hallowed be your name, but we are wondering why you still haven't came?
Give us this day our daily bread, if you can hear me please heal my horror filled head
and give birth to the dead, so the living won't die in vain.

Hands tightly together squeezed while on my knees with rosary beads that bleed,
listen to lightning strike as I recite the apostles creed.

It drips from my hands, blood mixed in with sand,
the same sand where Jesus left sacrificial steps.
Hail Mary full of grace, saying a prayer with blood smeared on my face.
Holy Mary mother of God in my final hour, blowing my last beautiful breaths.

Hands tightly together squeezed while on my knees with rosary beads that bleed,
listen to lightning strike as I recite the apostles creed.

Glory be to the Father, a prayer to make life a little less harder.
My physical future will not carry on much farther, my written word with no end,
it was bad back then, I pray for it not to be that bad again,
my brain, my mind, my soul, my spirit rise into the heavens and blend.

Hands tightly together squeezed while on my knees with rosary beads that bleed, listen to lightning strike as I recite the apostles creed.

Every word I spell, hoping they save me from a fiery hell,
save me from my sins, how much longer will it hurt me?
This feeling doesn't seem to be healing, an angel ailing,
I beg you master, for your mercy!

Hands tightly together squeezed while on my knees with rosary beads that bleed,
listen to lightning strike as I recite the apostles creed.

Hail Holy Queen as I drag you inside my dark dream.
Those who have said early goodbye's, I am stuck with their sighs,
forever stuck in my mind beyond the end of time.
My conscience forever echoing a city's cries.

Hands tightly together squeezed while on my knees with rosary beads that bleed,
listen to lightning strike as I recite the apostles creed.

Out of my eye falls a tear, the after rosary prayer.
To the begotten son from the forgotten one, I beg for a response.
The message I heed as blood drips from my fingers and continues to bleed,
a holy bloody rosary that forever haunts.

Hands tightly together squeezed while on my knees with rosary beads that bleed,
listen to lightning strike as I recite the apostles creed.

Joyful, luminous, sorrowful, glorious, I write, then I recite.
In between my legs a cup of my own blood.
Falling from the church ceiling, blood covered stained glass leaves.
A prayer hoping to gain the Lord's love.

Hands tightly together squeezed while on my knees with rosary beads that bleed,
listen to lightning strike as I recite the apostles creed.

A BEAUTIFUL YOUNG GIRL

What's wrong with this world
when a beautiful young girl dreams to be dead?
A lifeless body drained of pain,
the only image that plays in her head.

What's wrong with this world
when a beautiful young girl contemplates prostitution?
Not because of pleasure, but because she is broke
and this is the only job that is somewhat of a solution.

What's wrong with this world
when a beautiful young girl with piles of potential is a drug addict?
Her friends tell her she can sell drugs for them, but she
just gets high off her own supply and will never be able to kick her habit.

What's wrong with this world
when a beautiful young girl has a beautiful young girl of her own?
She hires dealers and addicts to watch her child when she's not home,
it's either that or have her daughter be all alone.

What's wrong with this world
when a beautiful young girl has no one to help her, only to hurt her?
She has people running to her with their problems,
but when she is in her time of need everyone seems to desert her.

What's wrong with this world
when a beautiful young girl cries for help and no one responds?
There are thousands of these beautiful young girls
and not one of them feels like they belong.

What's wrong with this world
when a beautiful young girl can barely even breathe?
Told me she has hurt so much

she no longer knows how it feels to grieve.

What's wrong with this world
when a beautiful young girl gets sexually abused by her dad?
He calls her names like slut, loser, tramp, bitch.
Is she supposed to go out into the world and not feel sad?

What's wrong with this world
when a beautiful young girl can't even afford any groceries?
What's wrong with this world?
I know this is not how it is supposed to be.

What's wrong with this world
when a beautiful young girl can't see because she has tears in her eyes?
No one cares about this beautiful young girl while she is alive
and no one will care about this beautiful young girl when she dies.

NATURE'S MESSAGE

Nature has a story to tell,
listen to the message being told.
The land we live on is neither Heaven nor Hell,
secret scripts are not always written in bold.
Whispers in the wind, pay attention,
people have many things to say, most of which is bad news.
Nature tells of truth ordinary humans forget to mention,
we search for answers and walk over clues.
Tears fall from the sky, making the ground wet,
the sun's smile appears to dry the rain,
a drop falls from our eyes when we are upset,
a loved one comforts to minimize pain.
Listen to leaves on a windy day, they beg for your appreciation,
they are cheering, giving you a standing ovation.

SUBWAY SCRIPTURES

8:30 p.m. and I'm on the subway
headed home.
Seated directly across from me was this guy
who had a Davy Crockett hat on his dome.
Seated next to me, on my right, was a man
with a horrible stench,
his sudden movements
made me flinch.

Standing up by the door, a man who was
wearing a trench coat and holding a briefcase.
Sitting down near him, an older man
with two sneakers and only one lace.

Against the subway driver's door
on a sign which read, PLEASE DON'T LEAN ON ,
was a middle aged lady
who had all green on.

Down the way was a man
who had more holes in his face
than Cornbread from *A Bronx Tale*,
next to him, a woman who had on blue jeans
along with a sweatshirt that read, Yale.

There was a homeless man in the corner
mumbling, "Is this how life is supposed to be?"
Across from him, a woman

who had eight bags full of groceries.
One bag was filled with cans of beer,
I wondered how they didn't tear?

Next to them, a young girl with black boots
fishnet stockings, a mini skirt and pink hair.
Directly across from her was an older man
who couldn't help but stare.
I could hear him thinking,
"Normal people are becoming very rare."

To my left, a hugely heavy man
who had trouble breathing,
and next to him was a gentleman
who had a burger and fries that he was eating.

The train had horrible brakes
and every time it tried to slow down
it sounded like people screaming.
A man passed out holding a bottle in a brown bag,
I wondered if he was dreaming?

We made it outside the tunnel,
hard to see the river because it was late in the evening.
It stopped at the next destination,
half the people on the train got up and began leaving.

The train descended back into the tunnel,
the lights flickered.
It was so loud that when someone had to talk

they leaned over, kissed the persons ear and whispered.

Across from me, a teenager with his headphones on,
I could hear the words the artist was singing,
an old school classic by Dr. Dre,
Keep Your Heads Ringing.

Next to him, a business man
who was checking his palm pilot
for some important appointment,
half of the people on the train made good money
and half collected unemployment.
The train stopped suddenly,
three people who were standing almost fell over,
half of the people on the train were drunk
and the other half were sober.

On the T there are
all these different characters I see,
as I sit waiting for my stop,
I wonder, who's watching me?

JUMP ROPE

While
the teacher stepped out of the room, a lesson
was being taught that would bring a young girl to her doom.

Students began touching her in the darkest places,
mean faces filled a swirling room.
They tore her shirt and stockings, threw her clothes on the floor
until she was wearing nothing more than sneakers with untied laces.

Their flailing arms prodded,
her knees stuck together as she crunched down
to cover up all she was revealing.
A few girls half-heartily tried to help her,
most laughed and snickered
as the classroom lights flickered.

Cell phones
caught the scene on tape,
footage boys
would go home to and masturbate.

Held by her hair,
sitting in the teacher's chair,
feet walking on air.
Nails scraping the board,
in a position where she could not be heard by the Lord.

Fingers addicted
to her shape,
no where to escape,
wasn't ready to give
what they decided to take.

The moment ended,
five boys were apprehended.

Diminished her worth

while leaving memories
which could not be murdered
once they gave birth.
Full of blame,
full of shame,
boys who erased the pureness of her name.

Later that night,
leaning against her bedroom window
listening to the soothing sound of rain.

Watching a leaf
slowly fall,
knowing she could never go back to school
and walk down those halls.
Couldn't live with the guilt,
the only way to sleep peacefully
was to tuck herself under the earth's quilt.

Hands underneath her skin
forever feeling her from within.

Tickling her throat with twine, underneath the moon's shine,
the only way to remove the scene from her mind.
Tied one end of a jump rope
around a pipe on her ceiling,
left a note
trying to
explain
what she was
feeling.
She then
wrapped
the other
end of the
jump rope
around her
throat.

A THRESHOLD'S WHISPERS

For at least a moment I yearn, to grab the knob and turn,
for just a peak, just a ponder, just a glimpse.
Afraid to stare at what might or might not be there, and in what form?
The door never opens more than an inch.

I don't want to let it out, what's still alive, what still survives.
The old chair still rocking, shhh, you can almost hear her talking.
Others come and visit, they can't hear the sighs
of her weightless feet on the wooden floor still walking.

Nothing in her room has been touched, memories blanketed with dust.
This will always be the room where she will sleep,
guarding the gate to her legacy, to me, she has given her trust,
an honor I will forever keep.

Most nights I sit against the door and lean, close my eyes and dream
of her coming out dressed in her robe and slippers.
I press my face on the floor against the beam
and listen to a threshold's whispers.

KELLY'S KID

If Kelly's kid was created by two people
who hated their lives and abused their minds,
what will become of Kelly's little girl as she grows up
and does not know of other ways to deal with tough times?

I don't blame the young man
and I don't blame the young lady,
it's not their fault
they were created crazy.
I don't know if there will come a time
when this wickedness will wither,
maybe it will be after a boy realizes he becomes a man
when he opens up his mind and closes his zipper.
Just because you see a pretty girl
does not mean you have to kiss her,
how can you say you love her
if you are not sure you would miss her?
You don't impress anyone, these days
it's much easier to open up the door underneath their draws,
as easy as it would be to go out every night
and break existing laws.
It doesn't matter if the laws are right, or
if the laws are wrong,
a father who creates a child and abandons it, teaches his child
they live inside a world where they will never belong.
Try to imagine growing in life
and feeling like a mistake,
blowing out candles on birthdays,
but were never meant to have a cake.

The courts have decided that on weekends
she can visit her daddy, to talk and maybe even have a meal,
no one loves him enough to pay his bail, they stare at each other eating

through the mirror separating them in the county jail.
Her father has been in and out of prison
for as long as she has known,
many men have come in and out of Kelly's house,
Kelly's kid has had a hard time remembering which was her own.
She grew up in a hotel for the hopeless,
every guy in town tried to make it their residence.
Kelly's kid goes to school, but her mind stays at home,
trying to figure out life, she could care less about learning past presidents.
A little food for thought,
if you believe knowledge produces power,
when Kelly's food stamps expire, one less lesson
and one less meal for her daughter's mind and mouth to devour.

I have been in Kelly's house, I know Kelly's kid.
The moment Kelly reads this
I know she will start crying.
I'm sorry,
but if I didn't tell,
the world would never come together and begin trying
to find a way to keep Kelly's kid from dying.
The truth hurts, almost as much
as the pain virgins feel all over the world
when they are too quick to lift up their skirts.
There is a single reason why
a young boy flirts.

The can of worms we call the world, I broke
open the cover and removed the lid,
a baby conceived corrupted
before it gets a chance to crawl out of the crib.
Another child is born and
another father has ran and hid.

THE OWL

Sitting in a cemetery under a midnight mist, pen clenched in my fist,
pondering my dear friend who had too young perished.
Wide awake from the moons glare, from my eye fell a tear,
directly down at his grave I stare, at a friend I greatly cherished.
Then, there was something, all of a sudden my shirt un-popped a button.
I heard a dog growl, I heard it howl, then I seen an owl who arrived and said nothing.

As I preciously recall, the owl did not make any movement at all.
Fog from the graveyard squalled, the horror came to a halt.
My strength was getting slender, you see, from the cemetery I wished to flee,
words walked off my breath, my friends death, was it my fault?
The owl's behavior, it did not waiver, still stood the earth,
believing I might be the reason my friend's corpse is buried underneath dirt.

Although I could not see past the fog's blur, I was sure, the owl and I, alone we were.
I did concur, who in their right mind, while alive, spends time where the deceased reside?
"Fly away," I plead! "Fly away," I plead, but the owl did not leave,
indeed, I started to bleed and I felt like I might not survive.
I seen the moment my friend died. I cried and puddles of mud became puddles of blood.
The owl stared with his scowl directly into my eyes and extracted every ounce of love.

My soul grew weaker, the night became bleaker.
I wiped blood off my sneaker and said, "What is it that you came to claim?"
It began to rain, the pain driving me insane, I took out a lighter and with the bright flame,
in the dirt with my finger, I spelled my friend's name.
As if the owl wanted to spite me, the owl slightly, nodded his head,
as the letters, C——H——R——I——S, out loud, I read.

Out of my lips, then out of the owl's lips came the name, "Chris."
The silence had been broken, the owl had spoken.
Inside the owl, could the identity possibly be someone who was a very good friend to me?
Lost in the darkness of the night, fingers crossed tight, hoping.
The conversation I was having, a dialog I couldn't fathom,

words only one other poet in history could imagine.

Two souls who were boldly brave faced each other by the grave.
With a whisk wave the owl tapped his toe on top the tomb,
waiting with respect with what would come next,
under the midnight moon, we stood amongst gloom and doom.
The obdurate owl observed obnoxiously and obsessed,
the invisible imagination of the owl was noticeably stressed.

"Chris," the name of my friend was spoken by the owl once again.
The evil eloquence of the owl's comments made no living sense.
The owl stayed on top of the tomb where my friend laid,
there I stood, head draped with a hood, facing a mystery that seemed immortally intense.
It was killing me, but willingly and diligently I paced back and forth trying to decipher,
the night seemed so long, but the sky was not getting brighter.

Maybe again never to see the light of day, the owl's fur ghostly gray,
quietly, it only spoke one word, yet it sounded so loud, the owl stood so proud.
The wise owl on a mission to make me listen,
both our bodies glistened inside the fog, it looked like we were floating on a cloud.
"Please speak something else from your lips!"
The owl's wings flapped, it almost seemed to laugh, out came the word, Chris.

In a circle I started to wander and proceeded to ponder,
that this, my friend Chris, was unearthly upset and unable to peacefully rest.
Somewhere in the spirit world he was trapped, on the dirt, the owl's shadow was cast.
Boundlessly and boldly off the owl's breath, there was something to confess.
Did the abrasive owl appear in the midnight air out of anger?
Was my facade familiar to the owl, or was I a grave stranger?

"Here I am! One man, in front of you I stand!
An explanation, a translation of your thoughts is what I demand!
Is your one word sentence part of your revenge or part of your repentance?"

The span between our spirits is not something I quite yet understand,

I stretched out my arm in frustration and like it was on command,
swirling smoke from the sand. It landed on my forearm, four inches from my hand.

What I observed ignited my nerves and made me want to vomit, amazingly astonished.
The leviathan landed and lingered. Carefully with my fingers, I padded the owl on its beak.
It stared into my eyes and much to my surprise, the owl wicked and wise,
more language began to leak out of its beak, another word the owl dared to speak.
The owl moved its lips and spoke, “Still exist.”
The owl moved its lips and spoke, “Still exist.”

I started to speak, but stuttered, from what the owl uttered,
something amazing I discovered, the faint familiarity of the owl’s speech.
The sound of my friend, it seems as though I have heard from him again.
Now it’s an idea that’s not too far out of reach, but what was the owl trying to teach?
In the twilight I was receiving a telegram from a transparent man,
but what was the purpose of his presence, and did he have a poignant plan?

I stood straight, the owl draped on my arm, not too far from the cemetery gate.
My friend who I thought was destroyed, now his presence, I again have awkwardly enjoyed.
Body tightening getting stiff, scene frightening like standing on the edge of a cliff,
a sign for all mankind that the vanished can come back from the void.
After the devastation of his demise, I looked to the skies, for this situation I have dreamt,
an owl who flew down from Heaven because it knew what it meant.

Back from an endless journey from all eternity, my friend has returned to me,
back from the annals of astrology, back to accept my apology.
“I hope you can still feel love and find it in your heart not to hold a grudge.”
The owl gave me a little nudge and I knew this tale was a moment meant for mythology.
The owl’s look of affection, the undeniable connection,
to my recollection, there was no doubt this was some sort of resurrection.

My friend stood on my arm in his new form, attracted to the sound of a heart torn.
My stressed out spirit stained with scorn.
Not responsible for his death, was the message coming off the owl’s breath,

the pain from my mundane mind, could this be a weight I no longer had to mourn?
The owl let out a yawn that put me at ease,
all of a sudden there was a rustling that came from the trees.

I carefully scouted, and then, “Shouted!”
The owl flew off of my hand, back on top the tomb where I first seen him stand.
Heavier, it began raining, from out of the darkness appeared a raven,
with its big black bold wings it flew next to the owl to land.
Out from the shadows appeared a second raven, who no longer felt the need to hide.
On top of my friend’s tomb stood an owl and two ravens, side by side.

I could tell they were allies from the look in their eyes,
in the sky, thunder and flashing light, I stared at an unreal sight.
Cemeteries are places of death, but here tonight, you could feel the power of life.
Myself, the owl and two ravens alone in the graveyard, in the middle of the night.
Truly something to behold,
from the dead to the living, a message was being told.

The soft spoken luminous language of the deceased, helping us humans live in peace.
The owl moved its lips and again spoke the name, “Chris.”
For years I shed tears as my heart fluttered with fears,
maybe because of me, my friend might not exist,
that was a thought that came nevermore as a raven spoke the word, “Lenore,” ever so slow.
It took awhile for the second raven to speak, admiring my style, it spoke with a smile, “Poe.”

LONELY LEAF FLOATING DOWN A STREAM

A slow fall as every moment
the leaf inches closer to the ground,
it falls into a river
and there is no sound.

The leaf burns with radiant autumn colors,
a fiery blend of yellow, orange and red,
it's caught in the current of the stream
and downhill it is led.
It is violently pushed and pulled
and thrown off of rocks,
it goes on forever
and never stops.
There is no turning back,
nothing to hold,
everything is moving so fast,
the water is so cold.
Leaves are supposed to live forever,
but this one's skin is
wrinkled and getting old.

It cannot go back to the branch with its peers
and cover up the bare bark of a tree,
never again be part of a beautiful picture
people stop to stare and see.

It is gone

and no one will take the time
to put it back where it belongs.
Never again know the home
where it has grown,
the place where it blossomed during autumn.
When you find the leaf
it will be washed up,
located at the river's bottom.

For those unfamiliar, the leaf's
beauty remains unknown,
wrinkled up and rotten, forever forgotten.
A lonely leaf
floating down a stream,
eyes halfway under water, blurry,
barely able to see its dream.

AN UNKNOWN ENDLESS ROAD

I
must proceed forward
toward a destination that is uncertain.
Step by step, embarking on a journey
that might cause great hurting.

This horrendous,
tremendous force pulls on my soul.
I want to turn around, but
if I go back now,
what I have been searching for
will not be found.

Without hesitation,
without reservation, I continue on.
Ignoring my inner voice and its opinion,
I walk past demons and devils
who dwell in dark dominions.

I do not look back,
I keep my eyes focused on
a hopeless sight
as I travel down a road
cloaked in night.
Red eyes stare from inside the bark
of bare trees, abnormalities in the air,
cold, bleak.
I follow my heart forward
even though I cannot see
the shadow of my figure

or the ground
where I place my feet.

I follow my heart
down an unknown endless road, calmly
trying to create
confidence in my character.
Wickedness whispering inside the wind
makes me wince,
I hear laughter.

I stand up straight
and follow my heart
to an unknown fate.
I follow my heart
down an unknown endless road, wondering
what will await?

THE NIGHT LOST

Five kids in a car,
turning on the ignition, music turned up so strangers could listen.
Bottle caps on beer bottles started twisting, sipping and passing.
Everyone was having a good time laughing and joking, sunroof open.
Kids full of potential and passion never thought of the car crashing.
On the way to a party on Saturday night, each looking for a girl who was just right.
Passing a blunt in the backseat and like a track meet, the car started to go faster.
The driver didn't want to risk humility, so he didn't speak of his inability.
Everything became still at 3:00 a.m. as they drove straight to their disaster.
The driver lost control, the car wrapped around a telephone pole, four was the death toll.

In the midst of the summers heat, bodies lifeless on concrete, none more than 20-years-old.
Results from moving too fast, broken glass, alas, this night would be their living last.
At the accident scene the wind is reciting the story being told.
After the smoke cleared, four peers sinking into a cemetery, overhead raining tears.
The one survivor has to live with cold stares, every night the moment reappears.
The moment before they crashed, four kids with bright futures became part of the past.
Every time a young kid opens a cold beer, their souls are released into the air.
One night of not thinking can change your entire world.
A bad decision left four no longer living and for one, a normal life stops.
This is the night lost.

I SWEAR TO GOD

God what the fuck!
Can’t you hear anything I say?

I have been asking for fucking help for years,
if you don’t answer me soon,
today is the last day I fucking pray!

Yeah, fuck that!
Pretty soon
I’m going to stop believing this religion bullshit,
I’m starting to think it has no meaning.

Fuck my values!
Fuck my ethics!
I try to live righteously,
but all anyone wants to do is fight,
I live a good life, but no one respects it.

I mean what the fuck is the point,
there might not even be any heavenly kingdom?
It might be all mother fucking lies!
I’ll never be able to hear angels singing!

If this fucking life is all there is,
I’m going to be so fucking pissed!
So much shit I fucking missed!
So many girls I could have kissed!

Crazy sex, drugs, stealing, killing,
living a life all out wild,
I didn’t do any of it,
I believed I was God’s child!
God, I’m in fucking denial!

I’m sick and don’t know if I’ll get well,
if there is a God,

sometimes it's so hard to fucking tell!
I swear to fucking God,
if you can hear me
send me straight to fucking Hell!

I swear to fucking God
I did all I could for every person,
but my situation would always worsen,
that's why God, that I'm fucking cursing!

I'm down here
drowning in your fucking rain,
that's why I am pointing my
fucking finger towards you with blame!

I swear to fucking God
I see demons while I'm dreaming,
no God, no angels, no saints.
Look at the life captured inside my books,
the picture that someone like me paints.

I swear to fucking God
you better show me a sign
that I'm not losing
my mother fucking mind.

I'm calling you out God,
Mr. Mother Fucking Divine.
I eat the bread that is your body
and drink your blood you say is wine.

Show yourself to me God!
Don't you think it's about fucking time?
You're hiding up in the clouds

while we're down here dying!
Those punk mother fucker prophets from the bible,
Moses, John, Matthew, Paul,
they were all fucking lying!

That's fucking right God,
I'm questioning your power,
your courage, your entire fucking existence!
I swear to God that if you showed yourself,
I would stop writing instantly.

I was fucking taught
to believe in you at an early age
and now I'm asking you to believe in me!
Stop avoiding and eluding me,
stop fucking deceiving me!
Show yourself God,
it's time for you to guide us with your grace.
Show yourself God,
show your mother fucking face!!!!

SWINGING IN TIME

She sat down on a swing listening to birds sing,
her beautiful brunette hair flared through the air.
A young girl without a care in the world swung back and forth inching closer to the sun.
This young radiant fair maiden with a gorgeous glare,
her feet so light, never touched the ground after taking flight.
Sun submerged out of sight and fell into night.

The sun rose like a flower, leaves sweaty from a nights shower,
the young girl rode the wind sitting on a morning breeze.
Never bending her knees, she kept gliding gracefully, innocently, playfully.
Silent rhymes came from wind chimes dangling on trees,
I looked out the window at a young girl, painting a picture with my brush
capturing a scene perfectly lush.

Days passed, she continued to sway forth and back.
The material hanging from the bottom of her dress swayed, the sky grayed.
Sipping lemonade out of a cracked glass, not aware of the dead grass,
she stayed for most of her life on the swing as everything around her decayed.
The swing slightly started to tilt, the flowers started to wilt, the swing started to rust,
the woman has now been diluted by a cloud of dust

settling a little at a time, I peeked out my blind.
Startled by steam screaming from my tea kettle, in my direction, she stared.
The swing stopped swinging, the birds stopped singing,
gray hair, glasses, wrinkles and age spots is now how she appeared.
I looked down at my hand and saw the skin of an old man telling the tale,
an image of what time decided to steal.

V

A young prostitute
sells her body for money.
Is she ever rich?

LEXINGTON PARK'S LAST STAND: THE BATTLE BETWEEN SOMERVILLE AND CHARLESTOWN

The summer heat
was at an all time high,
the night was calm, the air
was dry. The scene was the same
as any other night, Lexington Park
illuminated by one single street light.
Kids were playing basketball
while others hung out
on the long legendary concrete wall.
Boys trying to mack
pushed girls on the tire swing,
some smoked weed, drank beers
and did other illegal things.
Rumors swirled for weeks
that these Charlestown cats
were coming to our spot in Somerville
strapped with gats.
Lexington Park's fame
had been put on the map,
so much in fact, that people we didn't know
from another city were plotting an attack.
We sat, we laughed, we waited,
some of us sober, some of us faded.
This was the night it finally escaladed.
Cars sped down the avenue,
music thumping, kids yelling profanity.
The night Lexington Park
erupted with insanity.

We thought
they were scared to stop,
complete silence,
just as everyone shrugged it off,

out of nowhere, the violence.
They abandoned their cars around the block
and rushed us from all sides,
Lexington Park was the battleground
where Somerville and Charlestown would collide.

They didn't bring guns, but they brought
plenty of bats and hockey sticks.
The last thing I seen before I got hit,
hanging from a telephone wire,
a white pair of kicks.
We heard sirens
and all of us ran,
I must have landed a punch
as I looked at my swollen hand.
A few of us took cover
on a stranger's back steps,
licking our wounds
and catching our breath.
Hearts beating out of our chests,
looking at each other wide-eyed,
happy we escaped death.
Hours later everything settled down,
we went back to the park
and thought about the possibility of revenge
in city dark.

Truth is,
we never found out who they were,
kids from Charlestown
who attacked in a blur.
Because of the commotion
the city thought it was time to rebuild

and tear down the park where many of us
learned our life skills.
A place you could go
when everything else in your life
was wrong, a place where
you always felt like you belonged.

A week later Lexington Park
was demolished. Some of us went on to jail,
Heaven, work and college.
The same sneakers still hang
from their laces under a Somerville sky.
Lexington Park's last stand,
a moment in our neighborhood's history
that will never die.

I'M IN LOVE WITH A PROSTITUTE NAMED PATRICIA

I fell in love with Patricia
long before she started selling
her body for money.
She's still my girl
even though other men call her honey.

Patricia knew I loved her deeply,
she also knew her profession was slowly killing me.
Employed with a career that slowly destroys,
she was not a bad person,
only someone with limited possibilities.
When she was 12
her father introduced her to oral sex,
a true tale
with a moral everyone might not get.

Patricia's mom passed away when she was 13,
that was her best friend.
It signified the beginning of the end as
she became pregnant at 14,
had her baby at 15,
spent nine months as an expectant mother
and nine months as a dope fiend.

Needle-fed heroine
into her daughter's blood stream.
The baby didn't want to get high,
but when you're an embryo
no one can hear you scream.
A mother and an addict
who will never kick her habit,
it's the only way
she knows how to cope with dilemmas.
I can still picture it now,
a cigarette in her hand

while her body experienced tremors.
I remember being at the house
washing the floor and doing the dishes,
hoping that I could rejuvenate her mind
to once again experience wishes.

I could not provide comfort
for the entire day,
she needed to make her pay
and being a prostitute was the only known way.

I wish
I was the only man in her life
who got to hug and kiss her.
She might be a prostitute named Patricia,
but on my dresser I'll always have her picture
and tell her every night how much I miss her.

TOMB OF THE UNKNOWN WRITER

His life came to a tragic end
before we learned of the legendary man
who held the pen.

Why did he choose not to sign?
Masterful material
from a mysterious mind.
When will we discover what drove his greatness?
When will we learn what decided his fate?

His scripture was something to behold.
A man who wrote
some of the greatest tales ever told.

A man who knew
his end was near.
Prophetic perception
that brings people to his grave
just to stare.
His name still missing, alas,
the tomb of the unknown writer
and his suspicious shadow cast.

URBAN MONK

In a crowded city it is hard to breathe,
trying to inhale air so stale.
Mixed in with the breeze,
truth, lies, cigarette smoke and weed.
In a crowded city it is hard to believe.

Bare trees, girls on their knees,
the frail figures of drug addicts.
In a crowded city there is not much room to grieve.

Where does someone go to find inner peace in the streets?
Is there a place to experience tranquil thoughts?
I can't concentrate with sirens,
beeps and the homeless woman who weeps.
Where do I go when I can't escape my own heartbeat?
Running from my problems, from a broken family and from the cops,
no matter how pure, into my soul, sickness slowly seeps.

Hard to not walk in the same shoes as earlier crews,
easy money to make, hard to refuse.
Peers trying to convince me to be the same, I'm trying to change.
The effects of pollution and poverty, look at the sky,
it's no longer painted with beautiful blues.
Everyday the papers are reporting the same violent news.
It's in my brain, to fit in I have to wear gold chains
while gangs are my only real family.
I live in a society where there is little to gain and even less to lose.

It's time to be serious,
this is no time to laugh,
if I don't find a way out I am going to explode.
The cities wicked wind has me lost in its wrath.
This is the point in my life where I'm at…

While my friend is getting a gun to load,
I walk a different road.
I am an urban monk
who searches for a different path.

SOUND OF COLOR

A
shadow
is cast
behind
your
aging ash.

Cobwebs
and
dust
are the only parts
left of you
to touch.

In my room
the shades
are shut
tight,
I can't tell
whether it's
day or night.
The body bag
is
zipped tight.

A
soul
has smothered,
assuring tears
would be shed by
your mother.

From what
you had
swallowed,

forever
ended tomorrow.

Outlines
of faded images
are
my only memories.
I remember it like it was yesterday,
standing in
the cemetery.

I remember
sliding into my suit
which was
solemnly stitched.
Traveling
down roads
of dried up blood
which lined
my wrists.

Putting on
my
sunglasses
wondering about
the strange way
time passes.
I tried to
listen to the
priest speak,
but became distracted
by mascara
streaking down every
woman's cheek.
Watching them
carry you out of
the hearse,

standing in mud
which at some point
used to
be dirt.
Mortals,
spirits and lost souls
observed.
Eyes are closed,
vision
permanently
blurred.
As they lower you
into the ground,
over your casket
I held an umbrella.

On this day
I heard
the sound of color.

A BOY AND HIS BALL

A boy shoots his ball
long after everyone has went home, until no one else is around.
A boy bounces his ball
from when the sun goes up, until the sun goes down.

A boy cradles his ball
in his arms like a newborn.
The last thing he thinks about before bed,
the first thing he sees when he wakes up in the morning.

The ball could never be torn out of his arms,
the ball is there for his escape.
He kept shooting and dribbling
until he was no longer good, until he was great.

A boy and his ball together at the playground, it is his life,
to others it might just be a game.
It is how he is known around town,
the ball has given the boy his name.

While others are up to no good
you will always find a ball in the boy's hands.
The ball teaches and disciplines the boy,
it has helped him become a man.

He knows if he keeps practicing
he will be able to conquer all competition.
Throughout the neighborhood
the sound of swishing.

He shoots away his troubles until he is no longer upset.
His despair, with every dribble it seems to disappear
as the boy watches his ball, float
gracefully through the air.

A TALE OF TWO CITIES, 2005

In one city houses are surrounded
by white picket fences
with flowers growing freely on their lawn,
illustrate a picture of a perfect community
and this city would be drawn.
Freshly painted houses never chip,
nothing in this community could be tainted.
Doors stay unlocked
without bars on the windows,
if you get chilly all you have to do is turn up the heat
every time the cold wind blows.
People go to work everyday
accomplishing their goals,
they go home and eat delicious dinners
and always have extra butter
to spread on their rolls.
In one city people are selfish
and only watch out for their own backs,
but today they're going to take a trip
and see how people
live on the other side of the tracks.

Houses are falling apart,
people's sidewalks and lawns
are filled with litter.
Look around someone's house in this city
and it won't be too long
before you spot a tiny little critter.
Paint has been peeling
off houses for years,
drenched by acid rain
from troublesome tears.
People peek out of their blinds
to catch a glimpse of the sun,
parents don't let their children go out after dark

because every kid on these streets
either has a knife or a gun.
People stay in bed
because their desire is dead,
they only get up and go to work
to make sure their family is fed.
People get jealous
and crimes are committed,
the hearts that beat in this community are filled with hate
and it will never change unless
their spirits are lifted.
People from this city
have a harder time trying to make it because
the world believes
anything that grows here could not be gifted.

This is a tale of two cities
which takes place in the year 2005.
In one city people leave their house and live,
in the other city people leave their house
and hope to survive.

HEADING OUT OF CONTROL

Kerri lives on the street
behind me. She's 12-years-old with a figure
that's pretty plump and kinda chunky,
she stands at about 4'3"
so, she's pretty short and kinda stumpy.

Not quite a teenager,
but she is already participating in activities
meant for adults,
thinking sexy,
acting sexy,
looking sexy,
makes sex the eventual result.

Puberty hasn't taken over her body,
yet she has the ability
to make every 15-year-old boy's heart melt.
Her parents showed little affection at home,
Kerri only experienced love
when she was being felt.

I call her an entrepreneur
because she started her own business.
The name of her company, *How to Unbuckle a Boy's Belt.*
Right off the bat business was booming,
word hit the street
and Kerri experienced great success.
Called her the head doctor
because she was too young

to engage in anything, but oral sex.
Profits and penis' were rising by the minute.
Cash was the preferred payment,
her customers were too young
for credit cards and checks.

Down the street from her house
was an abandoned garage
where she conducted her covert operation,
it's the spot where young kids
from the neighborhood
would give in to pleasurable temptation.
It looked like a ride at a Disney World vacation,
with kids standing in line anxiously waiting.
At the end of the night Kerri was soaking wet
from sperm and perspiration.

Kerri is heading out of control
before she blew out a cake
with 16 candles,
becoming a pro, taking two customers at a time,
holding on for dear life to hard handles.
A dirty business
that will go down as one of the all-time top scandals.

GOD HEARD HER

Your face will always be remembered
through our eyes,
I wish I could take a lesson from you
on how an angel flies.
You were loved greatly
by the millions of your fans,
it is hard to understand
why someone so young
could have death in their plans?
Your special songs reached audiences
both young and old,
your elegantly spoken words
turned hearts warm when they were cold.

And so the story was told…

A sweet singing princess
was taken before her time,
it's not a coincidence
that your picture now reflects a heavenly shine.
Some things that happen
we will never be able to explain.
In our ears and in our hearts
is where you will remain.
The God's were looking for a beautiful person
with a beautiful voice,
when they heard Aaliyah
there would be no other choice.

A SLIGHTLY SLANTED, SLIGHTLY ENCHANTING BENCH

On the outskirts of the city's dirt and grime
is a secret place hidden by tall trees and twisting trails.
Put together with concrete bookends and rusty nails
is a slightly slanted, slightly enchanting bench I call mine.
It stands there and waits for me to arrive
after my hectic schedule which ends and begins again at five.
Painted with shadows, limbed brushes sketch over the sun's shine.
Leaves fall slowly from the sky without a chance to say goodbye.
Every time I come back I hear the same bird cry,
it saves me a seat, it knows I'm on my way.
The perfect place to end one part and begin the next part of my day.
When society tries to leave me behind
as the world moves fast,
this bench is where I go to clear my mind.
A lifetime elapsed.

WAITING…

Every morning at 6:35 A.M.
there is a woman who waits,
sits like a statue
with the same expression
on her face.
Extremely attractive, but yet
distracted.
Head turned to the side, she stares
knowing what she is waiting for
may never appear.

So still, so silent,
it doesn't look like she breaths in air.
Trees keep her company, leaves change
from orange to red, to yellow,
to branches that are bare.

Birds chirp, bees buzz,
this woman doesn't put up an umbrella
in the rain.
Snow plows growl, shovels scrape the pavement,
from those same trees
icicles hang, as
she continues to wait
for a moment that never came.

She keeps her ankles with no socks
and her fingers with no rings
crossed, her palms press down

on a mysterious brown box.

People sit down next to her,
she doesn’t acknowledge them,
she never talks.
The lonely lady sits on the bench
and continues to linger,
her brown hair blows in the wind
and on this little brown box
she gently taps her right index finger.
Patient,
contemplating,
waiting…

THE PREACHER'S DAUGHTER

The preacher and his daughter
lived on the campus of a monastery,
the atmosphere didn't allow her to be unique.
Unaware she would stick her finger
down her throat after a bite to eat.
The preaching father didn't bother
until he found out his daughter
did favors for a quarter.
Insides bleeding,
hanging out late in the evening
on the corner
of a street.
Left the house dressed in jeans and sneakers,
came out looking like Superwoman
after she hopped out of her pimp's back seat.
See-through shirt
and six inch heels on her feet.
Discrete and upbeat,
coming home looking flawlessly neat.
Felt the heat to make more money
working the beat.

Lost all hope,
you're saying she could still be saved...
Nope!
Started sniffing lines of coke,
giving head until her eyes watered
and turned bloodshot red.
Men didn't let her come up for air.
Choke.

Addicted to drugs, fake love and
the feeling of hot sperm
trickling down her throat.
Hooking up, hooked on prescription pills
and ends the day on her porch puffing
marijuana smoke.

UNDERNEATH MY EYELIDS

If there is no Heaven
where I get the chance to be a saint,
through my words I have created
a world of my own
with ink in my pen as the paint.

If there is no life
after death,
I don't want to spend
forever in the dark.
I might not be able to
open my eyes again, so,
under my eyelids I painted a portrait
of all that was in my heart.
I presume it will be lonely
once they bury me in a coffin,
mosaics of my mind
I will be able to view
while my body is deteriorating
and rotting.

My thoughts,
my journeys,
my visions,
to ensure my life
will not be forgotten.
I imagine death
to be like a dream

where you lay in peace
and view fragmented images
of moments with meaning.

No matter how much formaldehyde
they pump in my veins,
they will never be able to wash away
the portraits that remain.
Pictures of family who I have loved,
friends who I have specially selected,
great people in my life
who I have admired and respected.
Powerful, passionate, portraits,
painted underneath my eyelids
to ensure beauty in the beyond,
the art which I have perfected.

THE FADING MOON

Like a man without a home singing a sweet tune under a fading moon,
the center of my world is growling.
Heading underground hoping my ride will arrive soon,
my pupils looking for light, pacing and prowling.

My life starts moving, conducted by a sound which has become annoyingly soothing.
Comfort is not part of my day, so I choose to stand
near a young man with white strings that sing, his eyes closed, grooving.
Clinging to a pole, my athletically, aging, elderly hand.

The dusty bolder like books in my bag make my shoulders sag.
My cluttered brain, how much more information can it retain?
My fractured unfortunate frame I no longer wish to drag.
Inside the rumbling I hear a familiar voice, "next stop," call out a familiar name.

The doors swang open loud to a gang banging crowd,
who greet you with spiteful, sweaty stares.
Like a bull, making my way through the heap one by one as I'm allowed,
I step over sections of a broken mirror, skipping up subway stairs.

Not noticing how old I am becoming, the toll of all the running, I sigh without regret.
Slanting slightly upon my spot, back propped on a quaint wall, paint always freshly wet.
Standing alone next to a silhouette of a young couple dancing under an orange sky, and yet
no one else knows of the only place in the entire city where the sun will never set.

Selected Poems

of

Jasen Sousa

Age

17-24

THE UFC
ARTIST JUMP OFF
is now open!!
what we have:
2000 square feet!
various hip hop dance classes
mixed martial arts classes
full recording studio
womens and mens clothing
smoke shop
local and industry music
local visual art
DON'T MISS OUR GRAND OPENING HOUSE PARTY!!
318 SQUIRE RD REVERE MA 02151
myspace.com/unitedfrontco 781-520-1119

Save Our Somerville is a non-profit oranization dedicated to providing a voice to those who feel they have no voice in Somerville, Mass. Through community outreach, arts programs and support of youth events, SOS wants to strengthen what we believe are the dimishing community ties that make Somerville an ideal place to live.

FIND OUT WHAT'S GOING ON
IN THE WORLD OF JASEN SOUSA
OFFICIAL SITE
WWW.JASENSOUSA.NET
COMPANY SITE
WWW.JROCKPUBLISHING.COM
FAN SITE
MYSPACE.COM/JASENSOUSA
E-MAIL
JASENSOUSA@JROCKPUBLISHING.COM

What comes next will not be possible without acknowledging what came before.

J.S.